MASTER OF
CHILD
PSYCHOLOGY
INTERNSHIPS REPORTS

With Secondary School Children

Lim Lee Suan

PARTRIDGE

To order additional copies of this book, contact
Toll Free +65 3165 7531 (Singapore)
Toll Free +60 3 3099 4412 (Malaysia)
orders.singapore@partridgepublishing.com

www.partridgepublishing.com/singapore

CONTENTS

Acknowledgements

I want to thank God most of all. Because without God, I would not be able to do any of this.

Secondly, I would like to acknowledge the love, support and encouragement that my family has given me over the course of Master of Child Psychology. Thank you to my husband Jimmy for being there with unquestioning support and love. Without this I would not have made it.

I also would like to express my appreciation to all my lecturers from UCSI Psychology Department, Kuala Lumpur. I have gained more valuable insight into the school-counselling industry as a Master of Child Psychology student. Not to forget the principle, all senior assistances and other related teachers for their assistance in one way or another during my internships.

I gratefully acknowledge the support of my site supervisor, the school counsellor of SMK Taman Seraya, Puan Toh Geok Beh for her patience and dedication in guiding me. Last but not the least, I would like to express my heartfelt appreciation to wonderful counselling students of SMK Taman Seraya. I have valued our conversations and time together. Thank you.

Lim Lee Suan

Chapter 1
INTRODUCTION

Masters of Child Psychology practicum is a clinical experience being supervised and aimed to enable trainee student to build and expand basic skill of psychology and integrate professional knowledge to practice. Through these mandatory placements, trainees have an opportunity to gain something innovative to ensure the effectiveness of their professional services to the clients in school setting (Edwin & Gerler, 1992).

Organization information
History and type of organization

The organization placement for my internship/practicum is SMK Taman Seraya (SMKTS), Ampang, Selangor. SMKTS is a secondary school located in Ampang, Selangor, Malaysia. It was established in 1989. When first opened, the school is made up of four separate blocks. The fourth block was constructed beginning in 1994 and opened for use in 1998, when it was upgraded from Grade C to Grade A. Currently, SMK Taman Seraya has 1212 students and 105 teachers and operated between 6:45 and 18:45 each day. The principal is Encik Busrah bin Maulah (Manual Pengurusan & Takwim Pengurusan SMKTS,2020).

Mission, vision/ goals of SMKTS

School Mission: SMKTS strives to educate potential individuals who are capable to fulfill the nation's aspirations (*Melestarikan Sistem Pendidikan Yang Berkualiti Untuk Membangunkan Potensi Individu Bagi Memenuhi Aspirasi Negara*).

School Vision: SMKTS strives to produce highly educated individuals through quality education for the betterment of the nation (*Pendidikan Berkualiti Insan Terdidik Negara Sejahtera*)

Goals of SMKTS: SMKTS strives to educate individuals who are knowledgeable and competent, as well as being able to contribute to the harmony of the nation. (*Berilmu Harmonis Berbakti*)

Organizational structure

SMKTS secondary school adopted formal schooling system for children between age 13 to age 18. As an example of a formal organisation, SMKTS requires obedience to clear rules and regulations for goals to be achieved (Bozkuş, 2014) as they are influenced by the forces of the teachers, potential students and government policies (Schaefer, 2005). At the school level, supervision was normally done by the principal, the head of departments or the senior teacher empowered by the authority Thus, the role of school principal at SMKTS, En. Busrah bin Maulah is to exercise leadership, demonstrate vision, and empowerment with the assistance from head of academic department, Pn. Noorziah binti Kaliman, head of student affair department, Pn. Maimunah binti Mohd., head of co-curricular department, En. Mohd Jamil bin Abdul Hamid, and afternoon school session supervisor, Pn. Rohana binti Mohamed.

The head of academic department is required to lead, manage and develop the department to ensure that school teachers performance is managed appropriately, and fair workload allocation processes are in place among them since school teachers direct the learning of students on many subjects, including languages, mathematics, science, living skills, history, etc. (Dienye & Iwele, 2011). The duty of head of student affair department is to ensure it achieves the highest possible standards of excellence in all activities regarding students-welfare. It is also the student-affair department responsibility to ensure schools facilities and equipment are well-maintained, preserved and functional for the safety of teachers and school children (Ekundayo, 2012). Under the co-curricular plan of co-curricular department, focus is on activities involving sports and games, uniformed bodies community service, recreation and enrichment where formal curricula and practical experience are strengthened and expanded (Ab. Alim, 2004). The afternoon school session supervisor will supervise the curriculum implementation, improvement of teachers' professionalism, and all activities regarding students-welfare for lower secondary school children at SMKTS.

Practicum placement information
Department assigned

I am assigned to Guidance and Counselling Department of SMKTS under supervisions of school counsellor, Puan Toh Geok Beh. My main role is to assist remove class, form 1 and form 2 classes' school students (between age 13 to 15 years old) who need guidance and counselling services based on the identified needs of the respective students refer by school counsellors as well as other task requested by school administrators. The daily working- hours starts from 12.30 pm till 6.30 pm on Monday, Tuesday, Wednesday and Thursday, and it starts from 2.00pm to 6.00pm on Friday.

Role of the department

The guidance and counselling department of SMKTS plays an important role in developing students' personality development, career guidance and promote mental health wellness of students for transforming education, societies and economies challenges in 21st Century. According to Madam Toh Geok Beh, the main task of school counsellors is to plan and conduct psychological screening test and psychometric assessments to secondary school children throughout the year, follow by guidance and counselling program services based on the identified needs of the respective students on stress-related issues, behavior management, social skills development, career guidance and other identified areas.

Apart from that, counsellors will also provide consultation to staff in the areas of child and adolescent. They also provide on-going consultation to teachers, and support staff in classroom management and educational programming. Systems strengthening will be (further) enhanced in partnership with school Parent-Teacher Associations, government agencies, non-governmental organizations and other communities with a clear focus on promoting learning and greater equity of school children, and the realization of the Convention on the Rights of the Child – so that "Every Child Learns" (UNICEF

Education Strategy 2019–2030). The school administrators would provide vital support for the implementation of guidance and counselling program by allowing the time, facilities and resources to facilitate the process.

Job scope information
Job specification, duties/roles and responsibilities

My major job scope was to develop a work schedule with the Site Supervisor by following all required ethical codes and responsibilities in meeting Master of Child internship hours (240 hours in total). The internships also fulfilled the requirement of Master of Child Psychology training through preparation of the daily and weekly report/ reflections based on theories and development of children. My main role was to promote mental well-being among secondary school children at SMKTS. I worked directly with the school counsellors in assessing students with behavioral problems, stress-related problems or relationships problems, etc., by conducting individual/ group counselling, and arts therapy workshops. I also delivered guidance activities and others management and administration activities to the needs of the school.

Description of practicum environment

From my observations, I have learnt the importance of organizing proper counselling environment as a basis for a better counselling process. Firstly, the school counsellors have made students/clients feel more welcomed and ensured confidentiality in specific counselling room. The therapeutic setting of SMKTS counselling rooms such as comfort of furniture, lighting, and neatness, created a user friendly and emotionally safe counselling spaces for clients. The individual and group rooms with privacy and warm, intimate setting tend to produce higher levels of self-disclosure and more productive outcomes during counselling sessions (Pressley & Heesacker, 2001, Saegert & Winkel, 1990).

From my observations, SMKTS school counsellors created a collaborative relationship, opening up a range of possibilities for positive changes in clients. In these relationships, there is a climate of mutual respect and affirmation so that clients are free to create, explore, and improving their thoughts and behaviours (Duff &Bedi, 2010).

Chapter 2

WEEKLY REPORT

Daily log sheet (Week 1)

Date/Day	Task	Time	Learning outcome Skills acquired
20th Jan. 2020/Mon (12.30pm – 6.30pm)	Meeting school principal, En Busrah bin Maulah, senior assistances, school counsellors and school supervisor, Puan Toh Geok Bey	12.30pm – 2.30pm	Placement information - Department assigned - Description of practicum environment - Briefing about job task and duties
	- Online learning - Daily and weekly reports	2.30pm – 6.30pm	- Documentation - Reflection and recording of Chapter 1 based on research theories
			Total number of hours = 6

Daily Log sheet (Week 1 – cont.)

Date/Day	Task	Time	Learning outcome Skills acquired
21st Jan 2020/Tue (11.30am – 5.30pm)	Art Therapy workshop proposal	11.30 - 1.20pm	To discuss for submission of workshop proposal by next week
	Group Art Therapy (KK 001) - 4 Remove class, Chinese boys with disciplinary problems	1.20pm - 2.30pm	Adopted HTP art therapy – client awareness on issue at hand
	Group counselling session (KK 001-2)	2.30pm – 3.15pm	Introduce stress management coping skills. (To report to supervisor)
	- Case discussion with supervisor (KK 001) - Daily records and weekly report. (The effect of art therapy with school children)	3.15pm – 5.30pm	
			Total number of hours = 6

Daily Log sheet (Week 1 – cont.)

Date/Day	Task	Time	Learning outcome Skills acquired
22nd Jan. 2020/Wed (12.30pm – 6.30pm)	Discussion of referred case with supervisor (KI 001-1)	12.30pm – 12.50pm	Gather client's background information
	Individual counselling session with KI 001-1	12.50pm – 2.00pm	Adopted HTP art therapy & stress management. Client still suppressed with anger (To report to supervisor and child's mother)
	Reporting KI 001-1 case to supervisor and child's mother through phone conversation	2.00pm – 3.00pm	The mother and supervisor will monitor client's progress (To follow up during recess)
	Group counselling (KK 002-1) - 4 Remove class Chinese girls with peer relationship problems	3.00pm – 4.00pm	Stress management (To follow up during recess)

22nd Jan. 2020/Wed	Daily records and report	4.00pm – 4.30pm	- Documentation - Reflection ad recording
	Online learning - The effect of arts therapy with secondary school children	4.30pm – 6.30pm	- Documentation - Reflection and recording based on research theories
			Total number of hours = 6
23rd Jan 2020 – 27th Jan. 2020 (Thursday to Monday): Chinese New Year School Holidays			

Weekly report/reflection (Week 1)

Introducing arts therapy to secondary school children at SMKTS

I feel really fortunate to have my internship placement at SMK Taman Seraya. I have also met many influential people such as the school principal, En. Busrah bin Maulah, senior assistances, counsellors, and my site supervisor, Puan Toh Geok Beh, a very experiences professional school counsellor to guide me during the course of practicum/internships.

Apart from that, I also have the chance to understand the management of guidance and counselling programs, including areas such as planning, administration, and accountability. Additionally, it is encouraging to hear that the school counsellors are interested in conducting arts therapy workshop, as choice of interventions along with counselling sessions to help school children.

Arts therapy refers to a therapy modality which uses art as communications-bridge to individuals' subconscious mind. It is also defined as a mental health profession in improving overall quality of life (Malchiodi, 2012). According to Hoffmann (2016), expressive arts therapies have been incorporated into a variety of programs to improve mental health and rehabilitation by adopting stress relieving therapy for both adults and children, techniques vary depend on the clients' needs. Individuals would develop their sense of rhythm, musical imagination, physical and mental relaxation through specific music therapy. (Gold, Voracek &Wigram, 2004). In narrative therapy, individuals begin to view themselves apart from the problem, and feel more in charge of their life (Stillman, 2010). It is reported to decrease anxiety by integrating individuals understanding of the world (Arnheim, 1980). In affective symbolizing, arts making serves as a self-expression and emotion regulation tool on a personal and an interpersonal level (Geuther, 2015). For example, in House-Tree-Person (H- T-P) drawing (Buck, 1992), participants will be directed to draw experiences with family to provide reference points for discussions in the group. The experience encouraged individuals to think events that lead to positive experiences to enable affective and meaningful social life (Buck, 1992; Lakoff & Johnson, 1999; Mihalyi (1992)

Total hours (week 1): 18 hours

Supervisor's signature: _____   Student's signature: _____

Daily log sheet (Week 2)

Date/Day	Task	Time	Learning outcome Skills acquired
28th Jan 2020/Tue (12.30pm – 6.30pm)	Arts therapy workshop proposal	12.30pm – 3.15pm	Preparing to submit the following week
	Monitoring students progress during recess (KI 001, KK 001)	3.15pm – 4.00pm	Field notes (To follow up with KI 001)
	Group counselling (KK 003-1) - 3 Remove class Chinese girls with behavioral problems	4.00pm – 5.00pm	Stress management and communication skills training (To follow up during recess)
	- Daily records and report - Online learning (Effective of group counselling with school children)	5.00pm – 6.30pm	- Documentation - Reflection on practice and recording
			Total number of hours = 6

Daily log sheet (Week 2 – cont.)

Date/Day	Task	Time	Learning outcome Skills acquired
29th Jan. 2020/Wed (12.30pm – 6.30pm)	Online learning – The therapeutic of group counselling)	12.30pm – 2.30pm	Reflection on practice and recording
	Joint-case group counselling with supervisor (KK 004)	2.30pm – 3.15pm	Client's self-reporting documents
	Monitor students' progress during recess (KK 002, KK 003)	3.15pm – 4.00pm	Field notes (Follow up sessions)
	Group counselling (KK 001-1) - 4 Remove class Chinese boys with behavioural problems	4.00pm – 5.00pm	Stress management (To follow up during recess
	Daily records and report	5.00pm – 6.30pm	Documentation and recording
			Total number of hours = 6

Weekly report/reflection (Week 2)

The therapeutic of group counselling with secondary school children at SMKTS

This week, I have conducted few sessions of group-counselling, and monitor students' progress during recess through observations and jotting reflexive notes for reference (Leavy, 2017).

According to Rogers (1951), therapeutic group counselling contributed to self-confidence, feeling valued and relieved among group members (Corey & Corey, 1992). The most important task in group counselling is to establish and clarify rules or factors acceptance by the group members such as expectation of other group members; and a sense of security that allows members to be involved in the groups-interactions (Corey & Corey, 1992). On top of that, a circular seating is arranged during the group counselling to promote the exchange of ideas among members (Gladding, 1991).

Generally, after getting feedbacks from all members in counselling group, I would remind them to practice the coping-skills that they learned in order to control their behaviours. I would also remind the members of the next follow up session in monitoring their progress.

They might need to be coached again if they need further advice to accomplish their goals (Corey, 1990; Hansen, Warner, & Smith, 1980).

Total hours (week 2): 12 hours
Total hours overall: 30 hours

Supervisor's signature: _____   Student's signature: _____

Daily log sheet (Week 3)

Date/Day	Task	Time	Learning outcome Skills acquired
3rd Feb. 2020/Mon (12.30pm – 6.30pm)	Case discussion with supervisor (KI 003)	12.30pm – 1.00pm	Gather information for evaluation and reference
	Counselling appointment scheduled (KI 003, KK 005)	1.00pm – 1.30pm	Appointment schedule
	Individual counselling (KI 003 – 1) – Form 2 Chinese boy with behavioural problems	1.30pm – 2.30pm	Introduced anger management (To follow up by supervisor)
	Online learning – The impact of stress management coping skills among school children	2.30pm – 3.15pm	Reflection on weekly practice and recording
	Interview client's progress during recess (KK 003, KK004)	3.15pm – 4.00pm	Most clients showed significant improvement – no further services needed.
	Group counselling (KK 005-1) – 4 Remove class Chinese girls with behavioural problems	4.00pm – 5.10pm	Introduced stress management coping skills. (To follow up during recess)

	- Daily records and report - Online learning – the impact of stress management coping skills among school children)	5.10pm – 6.30pm	- Documentation Reflection on weekly practice and recording
			Total number hours = 6

Daily log sheet (Week 3 – cont.)

Date/Day	Task	Time	Learning outcome Skills acquired
4th Feb. 2020/Tue (12.00pm – 6.00pm)	Case document with supervisor (KK 006)	12.00pm – 12.40pm	Gather information for reference
	Group arts therapy and stress management with KK 006-1: 3 Form 4 girls (2 Chinese and 1 Malay) with family problems	12.40pm – 2.00pm	Adopted HTP drawing and stress management technique. (Follow up sessions by supervisor)
	Arts therapy workshop – a total of 38 participants from Form 1& 2 Amanah (8 boys, 30 girls) comprising a mix of Malays, Chinese and Indians.	2.00pm – 3.30pm	Adopted group art therapy and HTP drawing
	- Daily records and report - Arts therapy workshop report	3.30pm – 6.00pm	- Documentation - Reflection and recording
			Total number of hours = 6
5th Feb. 2020/Wednesday); Allowed to take leave with personal reason			

Daily log sheet (Week 3 – cont.)

Date/Day	Task	Time	Learning outcome Skills acquired
6ᵗʰ Feb. 2020/Thu (12.30pm – 6.30pm)	Case discussion with supervisor (KK 007)	12.30pm – 1.20pm	Gather client's background information for reference
	Group arts therapy (KK 007-1) – 3 Remove class Chinese girls with family problems	1.20pm – 3.15pm	Adopted HTP drawing technique (To follow up during recess)
	Interview clients' progress during recess (KK 003, KK 004, KK 005)	3.15pm – 4.00pm	Self-reported testimonials. Need to follow up with KK 005 showing progress with less significant
	Daily records, weekly reports and reflection.	4.00pm – 6.30pm	- Documentation - Reflection and recording
			Total number of hours = 6

Daily log sheet (Week 3 – cont.)

Date/Day	Task	Time	Learning outcome Skills acquired
7th Feb. 2020/Fri (2.00pm – 6.00pm)	Referral cases from counsellors (Form 2 students)	2.00pm – 3.00pm	Gather students' DASS-21 results for reference and evaluation
	Individual counselling (KI 004 -1) – Form 2 Malay girl with suppressed emotional problems	3.00pm – 4.15pm	Adopted HTP drawing and stress management technique (To follow up during recess)
	Group arts therapy (KK 008-1) – 2 Form 2 Malay girls with family problems	4.15pm – 5.20pm	Adopted HTP drawing technique (To follow up during recess)
	Daily records and report	5.20pm – 6.00pm	
			Total number of hours = 4

Weekly report/reflection (3)

The impact of stress management coping skills among secondary school children at SMKTS.

This week, I have conducted an arts therapy workshop and several counselling sessions based on screening of the Depression, Anxiety and Stress Scale (DASS-21) (Lovibond & Lovibond, 1995).

Being in their early adolescence stage, many problems confront lower secondary school students with physical, social, academic, and emotional adjustment. According to Smith & Lazarus (1993), anger could happen when individuals felt rejected and discouraged by others. In preventing aggression, I adopted stress management training program to manage students' emotion (Caprara, Regalia, & Bandura, 2002). The participants gained experience using visualization and relaxation techniques such as deep breathing relaxation and progressive muscular relaxation for them to practice in daily-basics (Motaby & Fathey, 2006c).

From the self-reported progress by the group members (KK001, KK003, KK005). 9 out of 11 students Felt relieved and happy after adopting the coping skills. The only two boys have less significant changes. Thus, longer term impact of the interventions would be continued towards lower secondary school children at SMKTS.

Total hours (week 3): 24 hours
Total hours overall: 54 hours

Supervisor's signature: _____   Student's signature: _____

Daily log sheet (week 4)

Date/Day	Task	Time	Learning outcome Skills acquired
10th Feb. 2020/Mon (12.30pm – 6.30pm)	Referral cases by supervisor (KK 009, KK 010)	12.30pm – 1.20pm	Gather information for reference
	Group arts therapy and stress management (KK 009-1): 2 Form 2 Chinese girls with family problems	1.20pm – 2.30pm	Adopted HTP drawing and stress management training. (To report to supervisor)
	Group counselling session (KK 010-1): 2 Form 2 Malay girls with emotional problems	2.30pm – 3.30pm	Adopted stress management and guided imagery (To report to supervisor)
	Reporting KK 009 and KK 010 cases to supervisor	3.30pm – 4.30pm	Supervisor will follow up with clients
	- Daily records and report - online learning (Psychotherapy and counselling	4.30pm – 6.30pm	- Documentation - Reflection on practice and recording
			Total number of hours = 6

Daily log sheet (Week 4 – cont.)

Date/Day	Task	Time	Learning outcome Skills acquired
11th Feb. 2020/Tue (12.30pm – 6.30pm)	Program discussion with supervisor	12.30pm – 1.00pm	Seraya Smart camp
	Counselling appointment scheduled (KK 011, KK 005, KI 006)	1.00pm – 1.30pm	Gather information for reference
	Group counselling (KK 011-1): 2 remove class Chinese girls with peer issue	1.30pm – 2.30pm	Adopted stress management (To monitor during recess)
	Individual counselling session (KI 005-1): Form 2 Indian girl with peer issues	2.30pm – 3.30pm	Adopted Solution Focused Brief Therapy (SFBT) – goal setting and exception questions To follow up next week)
	Interview students' progress during recession – (KK 006, KK 007, KK 008)	3.30pm – 4.00pm	To follow up with KK 006 since progress was less significant
	Individual counselling session (KI 006-1); Form 2 Malay girl with family problems.	4.00pm – 5.00pm	Adopted HTP drawing and stress management training Client felt more relieved (To monitor during recess)

	- Daily records and report - Online learning (Psychotherapy and counselling with school children	5.00pm – 6.30pm	- Documentation - Reflection and recording based on research theories
			Total number of hours = 6

Daily log sheet (Week 4 – cont.)

Date/Day	Task	Time	Learning outcome Skills acquired
12th Feb. 2020/Wed (12.30pm – 6.30pm)	Referral case discussion with supervisor (KK 005)	12.30pm – 1.00pm	Gather information for reference
	Group counselling session (KK 005-2): 4 Remove class Chinese girls with family problems	1.00pm – 2.00pm	Communication skill training (To monitor during recess)
	Group arts therapy (KK 012-1): 2 Form 2 Indian girls with family problems	2.00pm – 3.00pm	Adopted HTP drawing (To follow up during recess)
	Interview client's progress during recess (KK 007)	3.00pm - 4.00pm	Client felt happy. No further services needed.
	- Daily records and report - Weekly reflection and report	4.00pm – 6.30pm	- Documentation - Reflection and recording based on research theories
			Total number of hours = 6

Daily log sheet (Week 4 – cont.)

Date/Day	Task	Time	Learning outcome Skills acquired
13th Feb. 2020/Thu (12.30pm – 6.30pm)	Counselling appointment schedule (KK 005, KI 005, KI 006, KI 007)	12.30pm – 1.00pm	Appointment scheduling
	Online learning – Effectiveness of arts therapy among school children	1.00pm – 2.20pm	Reflection on practice and recording
	Group counselling (KK oo5-3): 4 Remove class Chinese girls with communication problems	2,20pm – 3.15pm	Adopted role play technique (To monitor during recess)
	Interviewing students' experiences with arts therapy	3.15pm – 4.00pm	Obtaining self-reported testimonials
	Individual counselling (KI 007-1): Form 2 Chinese girl with stress-related issues.	4.00pm – 5.00pm	Adopted stress management (To monitor during recess)
	Daily records and report	5.00pm – 6.00pm	- Documentation - Reflection and recording
			Total number of hours = 6

Lim Lee Suan

Daily log sheet (Week 4 – cont.)

Date/Day	Task	Time	Learning outcome Skills acquired
14th Feb. 2020/ Fri (2.00pm – 6.00pm)	Case discussion with school counsellor (KK 006)	2.00pm – 2.30pm	Gather information for reference
	Interviewing students' experience of arts therapy	2.30pm – 4.00pm	Documentation and recording
	Group arts therapy (KK 006-1): 3 Form 2 Malay girls with family problems.	4.00pm – 5.00pm	Adopted HTP arts therapy (To follow up during recess)
	- Recording of KK 006 case and interview sessions - Daily and weekly reports	5.00pm – 6.00pm	- Documentation - reflection and recording
			Total number of hours = 4

Weekly report/reflection (4)

The impact of arts therapy with secondary school children at SMKTS.

During the course of this week, I have conducted one particular Solution Focus Brief Therapy (SFBT) (Murphy, 2008; Sklare, 2005) with a client. I also conducted interviewing sessions with 10 students regarding their experiences with arts therapy to monitor clients' key changes of well-being. It also allowed me to review the effectiveness of therapy delivered (Lambert, 2010).

In psychology, the use of arts making approach to enhance mental health is known as arts therapy (Stuckey & Nobel, 2010, Wadson, 2010). Studies also found that artistic expression could considered as alternative interventions to promote mental health well-being among school children (Gersch & Goncalves, 2006; French & Klein, 2012; Mihaly, 1992).

Although arts therapy might be beneficial with clients, some of the findings on its effectiveness are mixed or inconclusive (Regev, 2018). For example, there were 7 out of 10 participants reported significant result with the therapy delivered. Thus, they should continue adopting coping-skills that they learned from previous arts therapy sessions. Alternatives of therapy or more time is needed to help the other 3 clients with less significant results (Haas, Hill, Lambert & Morrel, 2002).

Total hours (week 4): 28 hours
Total hours overall: 82 hours

Supervisor's signature: _____   Student's signature: _____

Daily log sheet (Week 5)

Date/Day	Task	Time	Learning outcome Skills acquired
18th Feb. 2020/Tue (12.30pm – 6.30pm	Case discussion with supervisor (KI 005, KI 013, KK 002)	12.30pm – 1.30pm	- Gather information - Appointment schedule
	Individual counselling (KI 005-2): Form 2 Indian girl with relationship problem	1.30pm – 2.30pm	Applied SFBT – scaling questions (To follow up during recess)
	Group counselling (KK 002-2): 4 Form 1 Chinese girls with relationship problems	2.30pm - 3.30pm	Implemented communication skills training (To follow up during recess
	Group arts therapy (KK 013-1): 2 From 2 Indian girls with family problems	3.30pm – 4.30pm	Adopted HTP arts therapy (To follow up in two weeks' time)
	- Daily records and report - Online learning – SFBT and school children	4.30pm – 6.30pm	- Documentation - Reflection and recording
			Total number of hours = 6
17th Feb. 2020/ (Monday): Allowed to take leave with personal reason.			

Daily log sheet (Week 5 – cont.)

Date/Day	Task	Time	Learning outcome Skills acquired
19th Feb. 2020/Wed (12.30pm – 6.30pm	Daily discussion with supervisor	12.30pm – 1.20pm	Appointment schedule
	Group arts therapy (KK 014-1): 3 Form 2 Malay girls with family problems	1.20pm – 2.30pm	Applied HTP arts therapy (To follow up during recess)
	Group arts therapy (KK 015-1): 2 Form 2 Malay girls with family problems	2.30pm – 3.30pm	Applied HTP arts therapy (To follow up during recess)
	Recording cases of KK 014, KK 015	3,30pm - 4.00pm	Documentation and recording
	Group counselling (KK 005-4): 4 Remove class Chinese girls (Follow-up session)	4.00pm – 5.15pm	Clients' self-reported testimonials and termination
	- Daily report - Online learning–Termination in counselling	5.15pm – 6.30pm	Reflection on practice and recording
			Total number of hours = 6

Daily log sheet (Week 5 – cont,)

Date/Day	Task	Time	Learning outcome Skills acquired
20th Feb. 2020/Thu (12.30pm – 6.30pm	Motivational program by HD Training House Sdn Bhd Kuala Lumpur	12.30pm – 5.30pm	Seraya Smart Camp for 100 school students – ice breaking, team building motivation activities. (Observation & reflection on practice)
	Online learning and daily report		Reflection on practice and recording based on research theories.
			Total number of hours = 6

Daily log sheet (Week 5 – cont,)

Date/Day	Task	Time	Learning outcome Skills acquired
21st Feb. 2020/Fri (2.00pm – 6.00pm	Online learning – Process of termination in counselling	2.00pm – 2.40pm	Reflection on practice based on research theories and recording.
	Group counselling (KK 016-1): 2 Form 2 Malay boys with stress issues	2.40pm – 3.40pm	Applied stress management training (To follow up during recess)
	Recording of KK 016 case	3.40pm – 4.00pm	Documentation and recording
	Group counselling (KK 017-1): 2 Form 2 Malay boys with peer issues.	4.00pm – 5.00pm	Applied anger management technique (To refer to supervisor)
	Daily record and report	5.00pm – 6.00pm	- Documentation - reflection and recording.
			Total number of hours = 4

Weekly report/reflection (Week 5)

Termination and saying good-bye in counselling.

During the course of this week, I have conducted six group arts therapy/counselling sessions with lower secondary school children. I also attended Seraya Smart Camp, a joint motivational program organized by guidance and counselling department of SMKTS, conducted by Ms. Chee from HD Training House Sdn. Bhd. Kuala Lumpur. A total of 100 students (30 boys, 70girls) have participated in the motivations program. From my observations and feedbacks from participants, Seraya Smart Camp has attracted attentions from the participants with creative activities. I have learned some tips of ice-breaking, and motivational strategies from the trainer. These include skills such as clarifying and checking perceptions, self-disclosure, where it add values to the participants' self-explorations, and summarizing content and process of activities delivered.

As for my experienced of conducting counselling sessions, I managed to terminate relationships with a group of clients, KK005 (4 Remove class Chinese girls with relationships and communications problems) on 19th Feb.2020, during their fourth-counselling session with me.

Termination is the term most commonly used to describe the process of finalizing or ending a counselling experience. This was commonly referred to as a follow up involved communicating with the client to ensure stability and well-being (Quintana and Holahan, 1992). The session encouraged the clients to share their range of feelings, both positive and negative, and relief that it is over (Bandura, 1977). In most successful cases, Quintana and Holahan (1992) reported that, clients discussed their feelings about termination, including pride, and significant changes can be helpful in promoting mental-wellbeing of participants. If the relationship was not established or the clients are afflicted by an issue that is beyond the skill of the counsellor, then the counsellor will refer the clients to seek services from another counsellor who is more capable to handle their issues. Thus, being able to recognize our own limits as trainee is important for the sake of affected clients. One way to do this is to ask clients questions such as, "Do you think you are benefiting from these counseling sessions?" Questions such as these set an expectation that counseling will end and serve to help clients prepare for the termination process. If there is a positive feedback for the client, the termination process may catalyze feelings in the counsellor of fulfillment, competency and even confidence. During these particular termination sessions, clients have conveyed a great deal of warmth regards to promote their self-worth with the coping skills they learned throughout the counselling sessions, and the successes they experienced as a result of engaging in the counselling-relationships. All in all, termination is often an ideal time that encourage clients to engage in active learning and reflection upon the counselling process as a new adventure in which they can apply the skills they have learned throughout their life. The end of counselling termination session, just like the end of a symphony as a resounding note that acts as a gateway to new beginnings of clients.

Total hours (week 5): 22 hours
Total hours overall: 104 hours

Supervisor's signature: _____   Student's signature: _____

Daily log sheet (Week 6)

Date/Day	Task	Time	Learning outcome Skills acquired
24ᵗʰ Feb. 2020/Mon (12.30pm – 6.30pm)	Case discussion with supervisor (KI 001, KI 008)	12.30pm – 1.30pm	Gather information for reference
	Individual arts therapy (KI 001-2): Form 2 Chinese boy with family problem	1.30pm – 2.40pm	Applied HTP arts therapy. Client experienced childhood trauma. (To report to supervisor and the child's mother)
	Individual arts therapy (KI 006-2): Form 2 Malay girl with family problem.	2.40pm – 3.20pm	Applied stress management technique. Client felt relieved. (To monitor during recess)
	Reporting KI 001 case to supervisor and child's mother through phone conversation	3.20pm – 4.00pm	The child's mother confirmed of childhood trauma incident and will monitor her son at home.
	Individual arts therapy (KI 008-1): Form 2 Indian girl with family problem	4.00pm – 5.00pm	Applied HTP art therapy and stress management. Client felt relieved (To report to supervisor)
	- Recording cases of KI 001, KI 006 and KI 008. - Daily reporting	5.00pm – 5.30pm	- Documentation - Reflection and recording

	Online learning – Childhood trauma exposed to domestic violence	5.30pm – 6.30pm	Reference and reflection on practice
			Total number of hours = 6

Daily log sheet (Week 6 – cont.)

Date/Day	Task	Time	Learning outcome Skills acquired
25th Feb. 2020/Tue (12.30pm – 6.30pm)	Counselling appointment schedule (KI 001, KK 018)	12.30pm – 1.00pm	Appointment schedule
	Individual counselling (KI 001-3): Form 2 Chinese boy with childhood trauma	1.00pm – 2.00pm	Applied stress management technique (To follow up with supervisor)
	Group counselling (KK 018-1): 2 Form 2 Indian girls with stress issues	2.00pm – 3.00pm	Applied stress management training (To monitor during recess)
	Online learning – Childhood trauma exposed to domestic violence.	3.00pm – 4.30pm	Reflection on practice and recording
	Case discussion with supervisor (KI 001)	4.30pm – 5.30pm	Supervisor will follow up with client
	Daily records and report	5.30pm – 6.30pm	Documentation and recording
			Total number of hours = 6

Daily log sheet (Week 6 – cont.)

Date/Day	Task	Time	Learning outcome Skills acquired
26th Feb. 2020/Wed (12.30pm – 6.30pm)	Motivational program by HD Training House Sdn Bhd, Kuala Lumpur	12.30pm – 5.30pm	Seraya Smart camp 2 – Team building and problem solving (Observation& reflection on practice)
	Daily record and report	5.30pm – 6.30pm	- Documentation - Reflection and recording
			Total number of hours = 6
27th Feb. 2020 (Thursday): Allowed to take leave due to SMKTS school sports day			

Daily log sheet (Week 6 – cont.)

Date/Day	Task	Time	Learning outcome Skills acquired
28th Feb. 2020/Fri (2.00pm – 6.00pm)	Individual counselling (KI 001-4): Form 2 Chinses boy with childhood trauma and online gaming addiction	2.00pm – 3.00pm	- Reporting KI 001 case to supervisor and the child's mother - Follow up during recess
	Group counselling (KK 019-1): 3 Form 2 Chinese boys with stress-related issues.	3.00pm – 3.40pm	Introduced stress management training (To monitor during recess)
	Interview KI 001 case to supervisor and client's mother	3.40pm – 4.30pm	Documentation and recording
	Reporting KI 001 case to supervisor and client's mother	4.30pm – 5.30pm	Supervisor will follow up with client. The child's mother will send her son for alternative training activities at home.
	- Recording cases of KI 001, KK 019 - Weekly report	5.30pm – 6.30pm	Documentation, weekly report, reflection and recording
			Total number of hours = 4

Weekly report/reflection (Week 6)

Childhood trauma exposed to domestic violence-a case study

During the course of this week, I have conducted a four counselling sessions and attended Seraya Smart Camp-2 conducted by HD Training House SDN. Bhd. Kuala Lumpur. I have also conducted a research regarding a case study on childhood trauma exposed to domestic violence with one of my client, Kent. (not his real name)

Kent is a Form 2 Chinese boy. I met Kent on 21st Jan. 2020 (Tuesday) for first counselling session due to complaints of being skipping classes and fighting at school. I have introduced stress management coping skills to Kent but he seemed still suppressed a lot of anger. I continued the counselling session by introducing H-T-P art therapy drawing to Kent. From the drawing, Kent told me how he witnessed his father hurting his mom while he was 8 years old. He saw her mom was breeding, and he was horrified and felt of intense fear. Based on my observations, Kent has experienced symptoms of childhood trauma exposed to domestic violence that kept haunting him since he was 8 years old till now (Kerig, Ford, & Olafson, 2014). Children who witness domestic violence often learn that violence equals power and control and sometimes affection (Holt, Buckley, & Whelan, 2008). Other symptoms include antisocial behavior, academic failure, and violent or abusive behavior in dating relationships, lack of responsiveness to rules and boundaries, and may frequently complain of headaches or stomachaches (Baker, Jaffe, Ashbourne, & Carter, 2002; Jackson, Cram, & Seymour, 2000; Rossman, Hughes, & Rosenburg, 2000).

During the sharing sessions, Kent admitted he couldn't control his behaviours since primary school. He also cannot tolerant with any schoolmates that triggered his anger. He would find fought with them to show his power. He also admitted he skipped classes frequently due to many reasons. He always rushed to toilet caused by his stomachaches symptoms. The second reason for him to skip classes was to meet her girl - friend from another class. And the last reason was he was looking for chances to find fault with his peers or playing on line games so he could release his anger and frustrations in order to free his mind.

After reporting Kent's case with my supervisor, I have been advised to discuss with Kent's mother, Lily for more information and justifications through telephone conversations. Lily confirmed with me Kent has experienced the childhood trauma, and he was staying with his maternal grandparents since both his parents were divorced after the incident . Lily also told me that she only meets Kent once a week since she was remarried with new family, but she promised she and her maternal family would tried to talk to Kent and monitor his behaviours at home.

At the last counselling sessions, after discussions with my supervisor and Kent's mother. I encouraged Kent to explore new behaviors of self-regulation to manage and release stress as important elements that forms the basis of successful intervention when it comes to trauma (Malchiodi, 2020; Beck, 1979; Nathan and Gorman 2015). Relaxation training has also become an important element in the treatment of children with anger management (Feindler & Ecton, 1986; Lochman, White, & Wayland, 1991).

Kent agreed to participate and explore new self-regulations life style in Kent's pleasurable activities such as playing badminton games, Chinese martial arts, (Wushu), jogging and helping his maternal grandparents to do house work to sustain any positive changes within Kent and allow the space for him to explore his own issues (Beck, 1979, Keegan & Holas, 2009). Thus, Kent's mother, school teachers and caregivers should provide a consistent environment and encouraging Kent to participate in these activities in order to cope with his life challenges. However, follow up counselling sessions by school counsellors are important to monitor client's progress. And professional assistance is recommended to the school and family if the child's response to the event does not improve in future.

Total hours (week 6): 22 hours

Total hours overall: 126 hours

Supervisor's signature: _____   Student's signature: _____

Daily log sheet (Week 7)

Date/Day	Task	Time	Learning outcome Skills acquired
2nd Mac. 2020/Mon (12.30pm – 6.30pm)	Counselling appointment scheduled (KK 020, KI 005)	12.30pm – 1.00pm	Gather background information for reference
	Group counselling (KK 0201-1): 2 Form 2 Indian girls with family issues	1.00pm – 2.00pm	Applied HTP arts therapy (To follow up during recess)
	Online learning – Arts Therapy research and practical guide	2.oopm – 4.00pm	Reflection on practice and recording
	Individual counselling (KI 005-3): Form 2 Indian girl with relationship problem	4.00pm – 5.00pm	Adopted SFBT scaling questions (To follow up the coming week)
	- Daily records and report - Online learning – Psychotherapy and counselling with school children	5.00pm – 6.30pm	- Documentation - reflection and recording
			Total number of hours = 6

<u>Daily log sheet (Week 7 – cont.)</u>

Date/Day	Task	Time	Learning outcome Skills acquired
3rd Mac. 2020/Tue (12.30pm – 6.30pm)	Progress discussion with supervisor	12.30pm – 2.30pm	- Planning parenting seminar for 7th Mac. 2020 (Saturday)
	- Daily record and report - Preparation on Internship report on Chapter 2	2.30pm – 6.30pm	Documentation and editing
			Total number of hours = 6

Daily log sheet (Week 7 – cont.)

Date/Day	Task	Time	Learning outcome Skills acquired
4th Mac. 2020/Wed (12.30pm – 6.30pm	Relieve classes as scheduled	12.30pm – 1.10pm	To collect examination papers
	Form 1 Dedikasi/ English paper	1.10pm – 1.45pm	Supervision of students in class
	Form 2 Elit Class/ English paper	1.45pm – 3.15pm	Supervision of students in class
	Internship report – Chapter 2	3.15pm – 4.20pm	- Documentation - Reflection and editing
	Form 2 Jujur class/ Chinese paper	4.20pm – 5.00pm	Supervision of students in class
	- Daily records and report - Internship report – Chapter 2	5.00pm – 6.30pm	- Documentation - Reflection and editing
			Total number of hours = 6

Daily log sheet (Week 7 – cont.)

Date/Day	Task	Time	Learning outcome Skills acquired
5th Mac. 2020/ Thu (12.30pm – 6.30pm)	Relieve classes scheduled	12.30pm – 1.10pm	To collect examination papers
	Form 1 Intelek/ Mathematic paper	1.10pm – 1.45pm	Supervision of students in class
	Internship report – Chapter 2	1.45pm – 2.45pm	- Documentation - Reflection and editing
	Form 2 Elit/ Mathematic paper	2.45pm – 3.15pm	Supervision of students in class
	Form 2 Lihur/ Moral paper	3.15pm – 5.00pm	Supervision of students in class
	- Daily record and report - Internship report – Chapter 2	5.00pm – 6.30pm	- Documentation - Reflection and editing
			Total number of hours = 6

Daily log sheet (Week 7 – cont.)

Date/Day	Task	Time	Learning outcome Skills acquired
6th Mac. 2020/Fri (2.00pm – 6.00pm	Relieve classes as scheduled	2.00pm – 2.30pm	To collect examination papers
	Internship report – Chapter 2	2.30pm – 3.30pm	- Documentation - Reflection and editing
	Form 1 Kreatif/ Chinese paper	3.30pm – 4.10pm	Supervision of students in class
	Internship report – Chapter 2	4.10pm – 5.00pm	- Documentation - Reflection and editing
	Form 2 Gigih/ Geography paper	5.00pm – 5.40pm	Supervision of students in class
	Daily record and report	5.40pm – 6.00pm	- Documentation - Reflection and editing
			Total number of hours = 4

Daily log sheet (Week 7 – cont.)

Date/Day	Task	Time	Learning outcome Skills acquired
7th Mac. 2020/Sat (8.30am – 12.30pm)	Registration of participants	8.30am – 9.00am	Assist in registering parents for the scheduled parenting seminar
	Parenting seminar conducted by Ms Chee Mun Chen of HD Training House Sdn Bhd, Kuala Lumpur	9.00am = 12.00pm	- Observation and reflection on practice - Documentation and recording
	Daily record and report	12.00pm – 12.30pm	- Documentation - Reflection and recording
			Total number of hours = 4

Weekly report/reflection (Week 7)

Online gaming and internet addiction among secondary school children at SMKTS.

This week. I have conducted 3 counselling sessions and relieved 7 classes during school- exam. I also attended school parenting-program conducted by Miss Chee, HD Training House Sdn. Bhd. Kuala Lumpur, on 7th. Mac.2020 (Saturday) and this event involved 20 parents.

One of the issues highlighted by parents was online gaming and internet addiction (IA) with their children. Parents were asked by Miss. Chee regarding parents' perceptions about children's internet use such as whether child neglected role obligations at home, or gave up social and recreational activities, due to IA. Most of the parents reported that their children spent more than 20 to 30 hours playing online gaming per week at home. Six in ten (52%) of the teens are using the internet more than 20 hours a week and about three in ten (26%) teenagers surf on a daily basis. These scenarios also reported by local studies involved adolescents under the age of 18 spent nearly six hours a day browsing the Internet (Malaysian Communications and Multimedia Commission, 2017). The attempts to reduce or stop IA are accompanied with restlessness, moody or aggressiveness behaviour to their parents or siblings. Parents also complained their children would isolate from their family and friends in order to play online- games, putting at risk to loss significant relationship, and educational opportunities.

IA or online gaming addictions of school children and adolescents is getting attention worldwide from health professionals, educators and society as it can lead to a negative impact including poor academic performance, social isolation physical and mental health problems to the exclusion of other events in life.(Wiederhold, 2016, Weinstein, 2015, McNicol &Thorsteinsson,2017). Often, online activities reported to be giving participants pleasure that make them unable to engage in real life activities (Bai, Lin, & Chen, 2001; Weinstein, 2015). Thus, parents were encouraged to establish very clear rules about online serving such as setting time- limits, and by participating in healthy lifestyle activities in order to get their lifestyle back on track.

Apart from that, parents also need to adopt positive parental skill and communicate effectively with their children. To many teens, they might not want to tell parents everything that happened in their lives, signs of becoming more independent. Thus, parents in return, need to adopt meaningful conversations with their children, at the same time, try to respect their privacy as young adults.

Other interventions such as Cognitive Behavioral Therapy (CBT) that involved cognitive restructuring, behavioural modifications or harm reduction therapy has produced significant results as interventions online gaming addictions or IA (Lee 2011, Young, 2009). All in all, there is a need for a holistic intervention within schools, teachers, parents and communities with the assistance of school counsellors to help school children with IA issues in Malaysia.

Total hours (week 7): 32 hours
Total hours overall: 158 hours

Supervisor's signature: _____   Student's signature: _____

Daily log sheet (Week 8)

Date/Day	Task	Time	Learning outcome Skills acquired
9th Mac. 2020/Mon (12.30pm – 6.30pm)	Counselling appointment scheduled (KK 021, KI 005)	12.30pm – 1.20pm	Gather background information for reference
	Group Counselling (KK 021): 2 Form2 Chinese girls with family issues	1.20pm – 2.20pm	Applied HTP arts therapy (To monitor during recess)
	Individual counselling (KI 006-3): Form 2 Malay girl with family problems	2.20pm – 3.30pm	- Self-reported testimonials - Termination of services
	Monitoring students' progress during recess	3.30pm – 4.00pm	Field notes for reflection on practice
	- Daily records and report - Online learning – Qualitativeresearch in arts therapy	4.00pm – 6.30pm	Reflection on practice and recording
			Total number of hours = 6

Daily log sheet (Week 8 – cont.)

Date/Day	Task	Time	Learning outcome Skills acquired
10th Mac. 2020/Tue (12.30pm – 6.30pm)	Group counselling (KK 022): 2 Form 3 Chinese girls with family issues	12.30pm – 1.20pm	Applied HTP arts therapy (To report to supervisor)
	Online learning – Qualitative research in arts therapy	1.20pm – 3.15pm	Reflection on practice and recording
	Monitoring students' progress during recess (KK 018, KK 019)	3.15pm – 4.00pm	- Clients were progressing - No further service needed
	- Daily record and report - Online learning – Qualitativeresearch in arts therapy	4.00pm – 6.30pm	Reflection on practice and recording
			Total number of hours = 6

Daily log sheet (Week 8 – cont.)

Date/Day	Task	Time	Learning outcome Skills acquired
11th Mac. 2020/Wed (12.30pm – 6.30pm	Group counselling (KK 023): 4 Form 3 Chinese girls with family issues	12.30pm – 1.20pm	Adopted HTP arts therapy (To report to supervisor)
	Online learning – research in HTP arts therapy	1.20pm – 3.15pm	Reflection on practice and recording
	Monitoring students' during recess (KK 020)	3.15pm – 4.00pm	Follow up session with clients with progress of less significance.
	Case discussion with supervisor (KK 020, KK 023)	4.00pm – 4.30pm	Supervisor to follow up with clients
	- Daily records and report - Weekly report reflection	4.30pm – 6.30pm	- Documentation - Reflection and recording
			Total number of hours = 6

Daily log sheet (Week 8 – cont.)

Date/Day	Task	Time	Learning outcome Skills acquired
12th Mac. 2020/Thu (12.30pm – 6.30pm)	Internship report – Chapter 2	12.30pm – 2.00pm	Editing internship report
	Group counselling (kk 020-2): 4 Form 2 Indian girls with family issues	2.00pm – 3.00pm	Applied stress management training (To report to supervisor)
	Monitoring students' progress during recess	3.00pm – 4.00pm	Field notes for reflection on practice
	Case discussion with supervisor (KK 020)	4.00pm – 4.30pm	Supervisor will follow up with client
	- Daily records and report - Weekly report reflection	4.30pm – 6.30pm	- Documentation - Reflection and recording
			Total number of hours = 6

Daily log sheet (Week 8 – cont.)

Date/Day	Task	Time	Learning outcome Skills acquired
13th Mac. 2020/Fri (2.00pm – 6.00pm)	Internship report	2.00pm – 3.00pm	Editing chapter 1 and 2 of internship report
	Monitoring students' progress during recess	3.00pm – 4.00pm	Field notes for reflection on practice
	Seeking advice from supervisor	4.00pm – 5.30pm	Final editing on internship report
	Daily records and report	5.30pm – 6.30pm	- Documentation - Reflections and recording
			Total number of hours = 4

Weekly report/reflection (Week 8)

The efficacy of House – Tree-Person (H-T-P) Test and stress management.

During the course of this week, I have conducted several H-T-P art therapy sessions. I also seeking advice from site supervisor regarding self-cares and career guidelines as a school counsellor.

Apart from that I also conducted an interviewing session on 9th Mac.2020 with a form-2 Malay girl, Farah(not her real name), regarding her experiences with H-T-P Test and stress management coping skills to overcome her stress-related issues with her family. House –Tree-Person (H-T-P) Test is a projective technique developed by John Buck (1992). The H-T-P Test is a two-phased approach to the personality.

During the first phase of H-T-P drawing, I directed Farah to draw a house, tree and person in one picture, implicates the rapport between herself and her family. The second phase of H-T-P Test, Farah was directed to describe the objects drawn, associated with her suppressed- feelings. Farah told me she was not happy with her parents that always quarrel at home. Her mind was disturbed, and could not concentrate on her studies. She also worried she could not perform well in the first semester school exam on Mac.2020. After listening to Farah's story, I introduced stress management coping skills to guide her, and remind her to practice at home.

At the end of the counselling session, Farah said she felt much more relieved. She also promised to practice the coping skills she learned, be more positive, and concentrate on her study.

Eventually, Farah has reached her goals and progressing in adopting positive coping skills

Total hours (week 8): 28 hours
Total hours overall: 186 hours

Supervisor's signature: _____   Student's signature: _____

Weekly report/reflection (18th March to 31st March 2020)

Reflection on my internship experience during Movement Control Order (MCO) period.

I have been instructed to work from home after Malaysian government announced a nationwide Movement Control Order (MCO), beginning 18th of March until 31st of March, 2020 due to the COVID-19 pandemic that has caused great distress not just in Malaysia, but also throughout the world. (Prime Minister's Office of Malaysia, 2020).

During MCO, apart from editing my internships report, I also keep up with my regular self-care routines such as gardening, meditation and cooking. These reminded me about my conversations with my site supervisor, Puan Toh with many occasions. We discussed the impact of our working alliance on our personal and professional growth, including the aspect of self-care.

Puan Toh explained that, she too had found personal self-care to be of considerable value in preventing burn out as a school counsellor (Bradley, Whisenhunt, Adamson, & Kress, 2013). One of her self-care coping skill is practices chanting meditation for her spiritual well-being.

From my observations, Pun Toh also presented as a sensible, personal and culturally competent in delivering her services towards school children (Noriah 2005). Research also suggested that if clients greeted by a culturally competent counsellor, they are more likely to respond positively to therapy and counselling sessions (Griner and Smith 2006, Sue & Sue, 2003).

Through this internship, I have also learned the importance of working as a team are relating to a great outcome. In working with my supervisor at SMKTS, I also developed a range of different skills for each of the platforms in guidance and counselling with school children. For example, apart from arts therapy, solution focus brief therapy (SFBT) might produce significant changes with some of the students as explained earlier in Chapter 2. Other aspects that I have improved through this internship are self-discipline, time management and work-life balance in order to get work done in an organised manner.

Total hours (during MCO): 56 hours
Total hours overall: 242 hours

Supervisor's signature: _____   Student's signature: _____

Chapter 3

CONCLUSION

Overview of practicum/internship experience

Field placement courses such as practicum and internship in school setting has provide opportunities for me to engage in experiences that strengthen my skills and techniques (Mansor & Wan Yusoff, 2013). During the course of my internships, I experienced a sense of personal growth and transition to working at the field placement site with school children at SMKTS. I also enjoyed building good relationships with my supervisor and clients, and that makes it more enjoyable.

Approached adopted during internship

Most cases handled during internship comprised a good mix of unresolved referred cases, emotional and behavioural misconducts of students such as low self-esteem, stress-related issues, peer-relations problems, bullying, truancy, and family problems. Since a good number of cases are related to emotional and behavioural issues, as being an school counsellor during my earlier career at SMK Seri Bintang Selatan, Cheras Kuala Lumpur, a combination of techniques were adopted for individuals or group counselling sessions, I adopted Cognitive Behavioral Therapy (CBT), breathing relaxations, progressive muscular relaxation, arts therapy and others related coping skills based on clients' needs. Implications for internships/

counselling practice. Good mental health enables school children to realize their potential, cope with the normal stresses of life, work productively, and contribute to their communities. Incorporating stress-related coping skills, cognitive-behavioural therapy along with arts therapy during my counselling sessions has shown significant results in promoting mental-health wellness at SMKTS. With this knowledge, school counsellors can better identify students experiencing excessive stress and tailor counselling interventions and arts therapy to encourage better relationships and community building (Councill, 2016, Linesch, 2016). The ability to communicate meaning in arts therapy as collaborative ways could work to address unsolved issues among individuals (Chapman, 2015, Councill, 2016, Linesch, 2016, Malchiodi, 2007). Since arts therapy is a mental health profession and one that involves a psychotherapeutic relationship, thus, arts therapy approaches in schools need to be conducted by profession trained arts therapists, clinical psychologist or school counsellors (Malchiodi, 2007).

Evaluating current models of arts therapy, stress-related coping skills, cognitive- behavioural therapy (CBT), and solution-focus brief therapy (SFBT) along with arts therapy in schools setting are also explained. On top of that, online-gaming addictions IA and its impact on school children is essential as explained in Chapter 2. These would require extensive research in different schools setting, including SMKTS for future researches to identify the diverse needs of students and the most suitable interventions that could work in respective schools or communities.

Research recommendations

Researchers in future are encouraged to proactively conduct relationship and responsiveness outcome studies with culturally diverse and historically clients at schools setting in Malaysia. On top of that, researchers are also encouraged to assess the effectiveness of psychotherapy with school children in future studies and reviews of "what works" in the therapy relationships (Norcross& Lambert, 2019, Norcross & Wampold, 2011 & Rosal, 2016).

Ongoing Consideration.

While I have gained much useful experiences at SMKTS, I feel that I still need to develop my skills and confidence levels dealing with cases of childhood trauma and online gaming addictions/ IA for my future undertaking. In my opinion, engaging in ongoing and proactive self-care as school counsellors is also essentials in order to provide professional services to communities and school children (Zahniser, Rupert, & Dorociak, 2017).

Conclusion

In conclusion, my experience with SMKTS was crucial in my development as a Master of Child Psychology student. I will take the lessons and skills I learned to apply them to my next position.

References

Ab. Alim, (2004): Pengurusan Gerak Kerja Kokurikulum. Selangor: Penerbit Oxford Sdn. Bhd.

Amato, P. R., & McInnes, I. R. (1983). Affiliative behavior in diverse environments: A consideration of pleasantness, information rate, and the arousal-eliciting quality of settings. Basic and Applied Social Psychology, 4(2), 109–122

Arnheim, R. (1980). Art as therapy. Arts in Psychotherapy, 7, 247–251

Bai YM, Lin CC, Chen JY. Internet addiction disorder among clients of a virtual clinic. Psychiatr Serv.2001;52: 1397.

Baker, L. L., Jaffe, P. G., Ashbourne, L., & Carter, J. (2002). Children exposed to domestic violence: An early childhood educator's handbook to increase understanding and improve community responses. London, Ontario: Centre for Children and Families in the Justice System. Retrieved 10 th Mac.2020, from from http://www.lfcc.on.ca/ece-us.PDF

Bandura, A. (1977). Social learning theory. Englewood Cliffs, NJ: Prentice Hall

Bandura, A. (2001). Social cognitive theory of mass communication. Media Psychology, 3(3), 265-299.

Beck, A. T. (1979). Cognitive therapy and the emotional disorders. New York: International Universities Press. Paperbound edition published by New American Library, New York, 1979.

Berg, I. K., & Dolan, Y. (2001). Tales of solutions: A collection of hope-inspiring stories. New York: Norton

Berg, I.K., & de Shazer, S. (1993). Making numbers talk: Language in therapy. In S. Friedman (Ed.). The new language of change (pp. 5–24). New York: Guilford.

Bozkuş, K. (2014). School as a social system. Sakarya University Journal of Education, 4(1), 49-61.

Bradley, N., Whisenhunt, J., Adamson, N., & Kress, V. E. (2013). Creative approaches for promoting counsellor self-care. Journal of Creativity in Mental Health, 8(4), 456–469 doi:10.1080/15401383.2013.844656

Buck, J. N. (1992). The house-tree-person projective drawing technique: Manual and interpretive guide (Rev. ed.). Los Angeles: Western Psychological Services.

Capara, G. V., Regalia, C., & Bandura, A. (2002). Longitudinal impact of perceived self-regulatory efficacy on violent conduct. European Psychologist, 7, 63–69.

Chapman, S. N. (2015). Arts immersion: Using the arts as a language across the primary school curriculum. Australian Journal of Teacher Education, 40(9). http://dx.doi.org/10.14221/ajte.2015v40n9.5

Corey, G. (1990). Theory and practice of group counseling (3rd ed.). Pacific Grove, CA: Brooks/Cole.

Corey, M. S., & Corey, G. (1992). Groups: Process and practice (4th ed.). Pacific Grove, CA: Brooks/Cole.

Councill, T. (2016). Art therapy with children. In D. E. Gussak & M. L. Rosal (Eds). The Institute for Public Health (IPH) (2015)

D.; Pontes, Halley M. (2018). "Psychometric assessment of the Internet Gaming Disorder diagnostic criteria: An Item Response Theory study". Addictive Behaviors Reports. 8: 176–184

De Jong, P., & Berg, I. K. (2013). Interviewing for solutions (4th ed.). Pacific Grove, CA: Brooks/Cole

Dienye, V. U., & Iwele, M. U. (2011). Education for value orientation in a multicultural society: the case of Nigeria. African Journal of Education and Technology, 1(3), 40-44.

Duff, C. T., & Bedi, R. P. (2010). Counsellor behaviours that predict therapeutic alliance: From the client's perspective. Counselling Psychology Quarterly, 23(1), 91-110.

Edwin, R. & Gerler, J.R. (1992). What we know about school counselling: A research to Borders & Drury. Journal of Counselling & Development, 74 (4)

Ekundayo, H. T. (2012). School facilities as correlates of students' achievement in the affective and psychomotor domains of learning. European Scientific Journal, 8(6), 208-215.

French, L., & Klein, R. (Eds.). (2012). Therapeutic practice in schools: Working with the child within: a clinical workbook for counsellors, psychotherapists and arts therapists. N.Y. and London: Routledge.

Gersch, I., & Goncalves, S.S.J. (2006). Creative arts therapies and educational psychology: Let's get together. Art Therapy: Journal of the American Art Therapy Association, 11(1), 22-32

Geuther, U. (2015). Körperpsychotherapie [Body psychotherapy]. Heidelberg: Springer. Gibson, J. J. (19

Gladding, S. T. (1991). Group work: A counseling specialty. New York: Macmillan.

Gold, C., Voracek, M., and Wigram, T. (2004). Effects of music therapy for children and adolescents with psychopathology: A meta-analysis. Journal of Child Psychology and Psychiatry and Allied Disciplines, 45,1054–1063.

Griner D, Smith TB. Culturally adapted mental health intervention: A meta-analytic review. Psychotherapy: Theory, Research, Practice, Training. 2006;43(4):531–548.

Hansen, J., Warner, R., & Smith, E. J. (1980). Group Counselling: Theory and Practice. Chicago: Rand McNally.

Hoffmann, B. (2016). The role of expressive therapies in therapeutic interactions; art therapy-explanation and concept. Trakia Journal of Sciences, No 3, pp 197-202.

Holt, S., Buckley, H., & Whelan, S. (2008). The impact of exposure to domestic violence on children and young people: A review of the literature. Child Abuse and Neglect, 32(8), 797–810. doi:10.1016/j.chiabu.2008.02.004

Keegan, E.& Holas, P. (2009).Cognitive-behavior therapy. Theory and practice. New York: Springer Publications

)Kerig, P. K., Ford, J. D., & Olafson, E. (2014). Assessing exposure to psychological trauma and Post-traumatic stress symptoms in the juvenile justice population. Los Angeles, CA and Durham, NC: National Center for Child Traumatic Stress. Retrieved 10th Mac.2020, from http://www.nctsn.org/sites/default/files/assets/pdfs/assessing_trauma_in_jj_2014.pdf

Lakoff, G., & Johnson, M. (1999). Philosophy in the flesh: the embodied mind and its challenge to Western thought. New York: Basic Books.

Lambert, M.J. (2010). Preventions of treatment failure: The use of measuring, monitoring, and feedback in clinical practice. Washington, DC: American Psychological Association

Leavy, P.(2017). Research design: Quantitative, qualitative, mixed methods, arts-based, and community based participatory research approaches. New York, NY: Guilford Press.

Lee E.J.A case study of Internet Game Addiction. Journal of Addictions Nursing.2011; 22(4): 208-213.

Linesch, D. (2016). Art therapy with adolescents. In D. E. Gussak & M. L. Rosal (Eds), The Wiley handbook of art therapy. New Jersey, USA: Wiley

Lovibond SH, Lovibond PF: Manual for the Depression Anxiety Stress Scales. Sydney Psychology Foundation Australia 1995

Malaysian Communications and Multimedia Commission. (2017).Internet Users Statistics in Malaysia. Cyberjaya: Selangor.

Malchiodi, C. A. (2007). The art therapy sourcebook. New York: McGraw-Hill

Malchiodi, C. A. (2020). Trauma and Expressive Arts Therapy: Brain, Body, and Imagination in the Healing Process. New York: Guilford Publications.

Mansor, N., & Wan Yusoff, W. M. (2013). Feelings and experience of counseling practicum students and implications for counseling supervision. Journal of Educational and Social Research, 3(7), 731-736. doi:10.5901/jesr.2013.v3n7p73

Manual Pengurusan & Takwim Pengurusan SMKTS (2020). Fn Smart Enterprise: Selangor Pressly, P. K., & Heesacker, M. (2001). The physical environment and counselling: A review of theory and research. Journal of Counseling and Development, 79(2), 148–160

Manual Pengurusan & Takwim Pengurusan SMKTS (2020). Fn Smart Enterprise: Selangor

McNicol, M. L., & Thorsteinsson, E. B. (2017). Internet addiction, psychological distress, and coping responses among adolescents and adults. Cyberpsychology, Behavior, and Social Networking, 20, 296-304.

Mihalyi Csikszentmihalyi (1992).Flow: The Psychology of Happiness: The Classic Work on How to Achieve Happiness.

Motaby, F. & Fathey, L. (2006c). Stress management skills. Tehran, Iran: Danzhh.

Murphy, J. J. (2008). Solution-focused counselling in schools. Alexandria, VA: American Counselling Association.

Nathan, P. E., & Gorman, J. M. (2015). A guide to treatments that work (4th ed.). Oxford: Oxford University Press. National Child Traumatic Stress Network. (n.d.). National Child Traumatic Stress Network empirically supported treatments and promising practices. Retrieved 18th Mac.2020, from National Child Traumatic Stress Network: http://www.nctsn.org/resources/topics/treatments-that-work/promising-practices

National health and morbidity survey 2015 (NHMS 2015). Vol. II: Non-communicable diseases, risk factors & other health problems.

Norcross, J. C., & Lambert, M. J. (Eds.). (2019). Psychotherapy relationships that work (3rd ed.

Norcross, J. C., & Wampold, B. E. (2011). What works for whom: Tailoring psychotherapy to the person. Journal of Clinical Psychology, 67, 127–132.

Noriah, I. (2005). Emotional quotient: Fundamental competency among counselors. Proceeding 2nd.Ministry of Education Counseling Seminar: Langkawi, Kedah 30th. May-2nd June 2005:165-181.65-76

Pressly, P. K., & Heesacker, M. (2001). The physical environment and counselling: A review of theory and research. Journal of Counseling and Development, 79(2), 148–160

Prime Minister's Office of Malaysia, 2020. Retrieved 19th Mac.2020 from: https://www.pmo.gov.my/tag/2019novelcoronavirus/

Quintana, S. M., & Holahan, W. (1992). Termination in short-term counseling: Successful and unsuccessful cases. Journal of Counseling Psychology, 39, 299 –305. http://dx.doi.org/10.1037/0022-0167.39.3.299

Rogers, C. (1951). Client-Centered Therapy: Its Current Practice, Implications and theory. London: Constable.

Rosal, M. (2016). Rethinking and reframing group art therapy: An amalgamation of British and US models. In D. E. Gussak & M. L. Rosal (Eds), The Wiley handbook of art therapy, p.231-241. New Jersey, USA: Wiley.

Rossman, B. B., Hughes, H. M., & Rosenburg, M. S. (2000). Children and interparental violence: The impact of exposure. Philadelphia, PA: Brunner/Mazel.

Russell, J. A., & Mehrabain, A. (1978). Approach-avoidance and affiliation as functions of the emotion-eliciting quality of an environment. Environment and Behavior, 10, 355–387.

Saegert, S., & Winkel, G. H. (1990). Environmental psychology. Annual Review of Psychology, 41, 441–477.

Saegert, S., & Winkel, G. H. (1990). Environmental psychology. Annual Review of Psychology, 41, 441–477.

Schaefer, R. T. (2005). Sociology. (9th Ed). New York, NY: McGraw-Hill.

Sklare, G. B. (2005). Brief counselling that works: A solution-focused approach for school counsellors and administrators. Thousand Oaks, California: Corwin Press & The American School Counsellor Association.

Smith, C. A., & Lazarus, R. S. (1993). Appraisal components, core relational themes, and the emotions. Cognition and Emotion, 7, 233–269.

Stillman, J. R. (2010). Narrative Therapy Trauma Manual: A Principle-Based Approach. St. Louis Park, MN: Caspersen, LLC.

Sue DW, Sue D. Counselling the Culturally Diverse: Theory and Practice. 4th ed. New York: John Wiley and Sons; 2003. Sociopolitical considerations of trust and mistrust; pp. 63–91.

UNICEF Education Strategy 2019–2030: UNICEF, [New York], retrieved on 6th Feb. 2020 from September, <https://www.unicef.org/media/59856/file/UNICEF-education-strategy-2019-2030.pdf>,

UNICEF Education Strategy 2019–2030: UNICEF, [New York], September,2019 <https://www.unicef.org/media/59856/file/UNICEF-education-strategy-2019-2030.pdf>, accessed 6 Feb. 2020Weinstein, A. (2015). Internet-addiction: diagnosis, comorbidity and treatment. Medical psychology in Russia: an electronic scientific journal, 4(33), 3.

Wiederhold, B. K. (2016). Low self-esteem and teens' Internet addiction: what have we learned in the last 20 years? Cyberpsychology, Behavior, and Social Networking, 6, 359-359.Young K. Internet addiction: diagnosis and treatment considerations. Journal of Contemporary Psychotherapy. 2009; 39(4): 241-246

Zahniser, E., Rupert, P. A., & Dorociak, K. E. (2017). Self-care in clinical psychology graduate training. Training and Education in Professional Psychology, 11, 283–289. http://dx.doi.org/10.1037/tep0000172